WHAT O'i n k k s AkE SAYING

Barb Tatlock is a strong and courageous woman who has battled the debilitating stronghold of depression. Her story is an inspiration to others who are struggling to overcome these conditions. She has learned many valuable truths and her story is a beacon of light in the darkness. It will encourage and give hope to those battling depression, as they endeavor to live a healthy fulfilling life.

-Paulette Winsor Holden

One thing I have loved about Barb over the years is her love of helping others in pain and seeing them become healthy. The compassion she lives by comes through her writing in a very honest and compelling manner. I love her willingness to be vulnerable in an effort for anyone reading to both identify with her and find yourself wanting to read more. In the Bible, Luke 1:78 - 79 we read, "Jesus came to put our feet on a path of peace", thank you Barb for sharing with all of us the peace you have found in Christ so eloquently. You have truly given a gift to all who suffer and want to find peace, health and wholeness for their pain.

*-**Christina Williams** Pastor of EngageOC, Irvine, California and Director of Elevated to Excellence*

A meaningful and honest exploration of depression from the inside out. This lovingly crafted book tells about Barb's journey back from the edge, and how she is becoming free in the Lord. Contains numerous bible verses and contemplations, written by someone that understands, that will be helpful to anyone suffering from depression, or those that love them. Highly recommended!

-**Coralie J**, Banks, FCMC, CEO, Leaping Cowgirl Productions Ltd.

In her courageous book "Living Life After Anti-Depressants - Emerging From the Shadows of the Vault", author Barb Tatlock shares her story of suffering, faith and healing, with the intent to help others. Specifically, it is for the many individuals being held hostage by stuffed emotions and the long term use of anti-depressants, to keep them that way.
Barbs insights in her book will inspire and shed light for those of us living and struggling with "Shadows".

-**Brian Lukyn**
-Author of **The Un-Retirement Guide TM**

Sharing from a vulnerable place, Barb takes you on her journey of living life with anti-depressants. When she faced the deeper truth that she could choose life or death, it was in choosing life that allowed her to step beyond anti-depressants and thrive. If depression is an area that you struggle with, you will find hope and healing through Living Life After Anti-Depressants. I highly recommend her book.

-**Linda Olson**, CEO, Christian Speakers Get paid
-Amazon #1 Bestseller, Uncovering the Champion Within

"Living Life After Anti-Depressants – Emerging From the Shadows of the Vault" is filled with expectant hope and timely examples for everyone who finds themselves walking through the valley of depression. Barb writes in such a personal way that you feel as though you are sitting down with a close friend who sincerely cares and understands. Her vulnerability and openness create a deep sense of safety, allowing you to be unguarded with your own struggles, while discovering a pathway towards your own health, healing and hope.

-**Barry Marsten**, Lead Pastor, Cornerstone Church

Trying to come off anti-depressants is one of the hardest things to be able to do. It is not only the drug coming out of your system, but dealing with the reasons why you went on it in the first place. Barb writes about her journey and creates hope and encouragement for those struggling with this as well. She shows that there is life after anti-depressants. Amen!

- **Dawnie McElligott**, RMT

This book will touch the heart and lives of many. Barb writes with such authenticity about her own journey of coming off anti-depressants. She articulates beautifully her daily walk of courage toward healing. It is in the difficulties of the journey that she finds true hope and self-acceptance. This book serves to encourage anyone who has ever lived with the impossible but dares to believe there is more.

- **Susan Z. Hastie**, MA, CCPS, CSAT (Candidate)

She will draw you into her story and leave you feeling hopeful and enlightened. I know you will leave the pages of this book refreshed and determined to help yourself or others move past the pain and into the life you were destined to live.

- **Kathleen D. Mailer**, International Business Evangelist; #1 Best Selling Author including, "*Walking In The Wake of the Holy Spirit, Living An Ordinary Life With An Extraordinary God*"; Editor-In-Chief of Today's Businesswoman Magazine

LIVING LIFE AFTER ANTI-DEPRESSANTS

Emerging From the Shadows of the Vault

By Barb Tatlock

DEDICATION

This book is dedicated to my Lord and Savior Jesus Christ, Son of the living God.

Without my relationship with Him and the direction and comfort of the Holy Spirit this journey would have been next to impossible.

I give all honor and glory to Him for His healing in my life and for giving me the ability to walk forward in this newness of life.

My heart is Yours, Lord.

ACKNOWLEDGEMENTS

I would love to acknowledge all those who have helped me on my journey; either knowingly or unknowingly.

First and foremost I want to thank my Lord and Saviour, Jesus Christ, for His all-sufficient love, grace and strength that have seen me through this process.

It is with a heart full of love and gratitude that I thank my awesome husband, Garry. Honey, you are the glue that holds me together and the wind beneath my wings. Your unflagging belief in me made this all possible. I will never be able to thank you enough – you have my heart now and always!

My heart-felt thanks go to my counsellor, Susan Z. Hastie, and my medical doctor, Dr. Ted Vant.

I need to thank Lysa TerKeurst and her team at Proverbs 31 Ministries for all the timely devotionals. It's hard to believe how they hit the nail on the head on almost any given day. The team at Faith Gateway has also been amazing with their timely devotionals. Both organizations have made this journey significantly easier than it might otherwise have been. Thank you!

TABLE OF CONTENTS

PREFACE

The idea for writing this book came to me as I was going through the agonies of withdrawal from anti-depressants. I felt like I was at the bottom of the bottomless pit, yet I knew if I could encourage one person the journey would be worth it. So in the midst of what felt like a whirlwind, a tsunami and a tornado all going on in my life all at once, this book was born. I have been as honest as I know how as I have shared my devastations and my healing.

I have written in such a way that you, the reader, will firstly get the story of my journey. Part of me trying to be open and honest is the inclusion of my journal pages from that time. I wanted to make sure that you would understand that this particular journey does not have a definitive end point but, rather, that it is a journey that will continue to the end of my days.

The second part gives some guidelines and strategies that helped me during this journey of coming off anti-depressants and I felt they might assist you on your journey, should you choose to undertake it. Should you choose to stay on anti-depressants the strategies I outlined will still help you to live a fuller more victorious life.

Please get medical advice before making changes to any medications you may be on and be sure that you have a strong support system in place.

Part One

My Story

INTRODUCTION

Have you ever wondered what is behind a double reinforced steel door? Let me tell you. In my life it is a bank vault filled with safety deposit boxes. Some large, some medium and some small; all locked and then locked again behind the double reinforced steel door.

What is so important in my life, you might ask, that I require all those safety deposit boxes; locked up and neatly stored in a locked vault? I'll tell you a secret...those boxes are filled with memories of events and devastations that took place. Things that, in my own self-sufficiency, I was only able to lock away, in order to survive.

My Story

Chapter One

I would rather live than merely survive! Although survival is much less painful (can we say numbing), living is exhilarating and purposeful.

Deuteronomy 30:19-20 states: *I call heaven and earth as witnesses today against you, that I have set before you life and death, blessing and cursing; therefore choose life that both you and your descendants may live; that you may love the Lord your God, that you may obey His voice and that you might cling to Him, for He is your life and the length of your days.*

I chose survival for a long time – at least the last 60 years, and it has only been the last little while that I have chosen life rather than just survival. What a ride it has been!

You see I spent the last 24 years of my life on anti-depressants because I couldn't deal with life by myself any longer. I was a Christian, but I didn't realize that God didn't want me to deal with everything by myself. God actually wanted to help me deal with the traumas, hurts and disappointments of life but I didn't know how to let Him do that. So in my own self-sufficiency, I put them into "safety deposit boxes" locked them nicely and securely and then put them into a "bank vault" in my mind. I locked that bank vault very securely, as I did not want the contents of those boxes raising their ugly little heads and causing me pain. That worked well until November 2014, when my "bank vault" started to pop its rivets. (I thought they were made stronger than that☺!)

The analogy of the safety deposit boxes and the bank vault came from a picture that the Lord gave me so that I would understand what I had done. Locking things away was a survival mechanism.

It did help me to survive, but it also put me in a place of deep depression, where I contemplated suicide several times. In this place of depression the only thing I felt I could do was to keep on locking things up. And so...locking things away became a way of life for me, until God showed me a different way of dealing with life.

IT IS COMING

Chapter Two

In September 2013, I had to euthanize my faithful companion of 13 years, Sassy. She was a Jack Russell cross and she was the funniest little thing. She made me laugh at least once a day. (That was the condition of me adopting her!) However, when she developed kidney failure I couldn't keep her alive when she was in pain.

Next, in November 2013, my Mom died at the ripe old age of 96. We had a very close relationship, almost to the point of co-dependency, so her death was a very hard time for me. I put a lot of that pain into a "safety deposit box" and told myself it was okay because she really did want to go home to be with the Lord and I really just wanted her to be happy, so I *needed* to be okay and even rejoice when her wish finally came true.

Then, in August 2014, I had a very dear friend die of cancer. I had stood firm with her, believing for divine healing, for over 2 years. When she died it was like I lost a part of myself. Again, I told myself that she was in a much better place and that I couldn't really grieve for her as she had made peace with her death before she passed. But, I didn't allow myself to grieve for me, either.

Do you see how emotions can get compressed and build up over time? Those 3 increasingly stuffed "safety deposit boxes" were a big part of what caused my "bank vault" to pop its rivets.

Finally, my sister and I went to Ontario for our niece's wedding and that is where things came to a head for me. You see, my brother had been killed in a car accident in 1982 and I became like a surrogate parent to my niece and nephew and was very close to my sister-in-law. In 1984 my sister-in-law decided to move back to Ontario, where she was from. When she moved to Ontario, she slowly but surely drew further and further away from me until there was no connection at all. This absolutely broke my heart, but as time went on I thought I had dealt with it because I had gotten to the point of forgiving her for taking my niece and nephew and moving back east.

To make a long story short, 3 years before the wedding, my niece got in touch with my sister and me. She came out for a visit and we reconnected.

The day my sister and I arrived in Ontario for the wedding, the four of us, (my niece, sister-in-law, sister and I) sat down to have coffee. It was then that things started to shift for me.

My sister-in-law apologized for distancing herself from us for so long and she admitted that she had never dealt with my brother's death until 3 years ago. I sat there in stunned wonder, thinking to myself, "How could you not possibly deal with his death for almost 30 years? Are you kidding me?!?!" Remember, I thought I had dealt with all this stuff already.

Reality hit and it hit hard. **That** is when God started to deal with me about my "bank vault" and all my little and not so little "safety deposit boxes". It wasn't a tidal wave of revelation; our God is too compassionate for that, but just a very slow popping of the rivets off the "bank vault". Because, once I accepted the fact that I had one unhealed hurt, my brother's death, all the rest of my unhealed past started clamoring for attention. I found that I wasn't sleeping well and that I felt panicky a good part of the time (shortness of breath and rapid heartbeat). I had no energy and life was overwhelming. I didn't know which way to turn but at the same time I couldn't put my finger on what was wrong.

So in November of 2014 my "bank vault" of memories started to pop its rivets as the anti-depressants I was on were no longer working effectively.

It was finally my husband who suggested perhaps my medications needed to be adjusted. We were lying in bed one morning and I looked at him as I was crying and said, "I don't know what is wrong with me."

His response was, "Maybe you need and adjustment."

I said, "What, an attitude adjustment?"

He just smiled and said, "No."

So I then asked, "What, a chiropractic adjustment?"

Again he just smiled and said, "No."

Well by now I was really confused and I said to him, "Honey, I'm really not getting this; you're gonna have to spell out for me what you mean."

That is when he very gently said: "You are going to the doctor tomorrow, right? I think your meds might need to be adjusted."

You could have knocked me over with a feather! That thought hadn't even entered my mind! I went to my physician the next day, I just happened to have an appointment for something else, and for the next two and one-half months we tried playing with the doses of the anti-depressants (Effexor and Wellbutrin) that I was on; all to no avail.

The Bank Vault
Pops its Rivets

Chapter Two

The end of January I decided to start some counselling and it's a good thing I did, because on February 4th, 2015 my doctor and I decided that a change of medications was in order. My doctor really didn't want to do that because I was already in crisis, but he saw no other option and serious times call for serious measures. In order to accomplish this, we decided that I would have to wean myself off of both the anti-depressants I was on first. Then we would try a new, perhaps more effective medication.

One of the first things that God revealed to me in my first counselling session was that I had never really grieved for the people I had lost in my life. My counsellor explained to me that allowing myself to grieve for someone was, and is, like the last gift I could give them.

The grieving process would allow me to show them how much they meant to me and the impact they had on my life. It would allow me to express just how much I would miss them and the gaping hole that they had left in my life.

So my homework that week was to allow myself to grieve for those I had lost. Obviously that didn't happen all at once but at least I got started! It felt like hard work, and here I thought grieving was for wussies!

That Sunday was when God showed me what I did with my hurts, griefs and traumas. It was then that He revealed the "safety deposit box" and "bank vault" analogy.

At my next appointment I told my counsellor about the analogy of the safety deposit boxes and the bank vault. The first exercise she gave me to do was this: She found a picture on the internet of an open bank vault with all the safety deposit boxes in it and she asked me if I would take it home and start labeling the boxes as the Lord revealed to me what I had hidden. Wow! All I can say is that it wasn't pretty.

My rack of safety deposit boxes read something like this:

1. Mom and Dad not wanting me when they found out Mom was pregnant. (They didn't know how they were going to feed another child.)

2. Being pushed down the stairs by my baby-sitter when I was little because I wasn't fast enough.

3. I was molested by another baby-sitter when I was 8 years old.

4. Being left home from holidays because I was sick. Now before you start thinking my parents were awful, I actually volunteered to stay home because I didn't want anybody to miss out on holidays and I really liked the boy next door who was going to be my sitter. You got it: The same one who molested me.

5. Daddy breaking a promise after I had broken my leg. He promised to take me to a drive-in but his boss came into town.

6. Moving to Vancouver and leaving all my friends behind. This was tough because our family was one of the first families in Sherwood Park and each time a new child moved into our neighborhood, they had to come into my friend group. I had never, before our move, had to fit into a group or make new friends where I was the outsider.

7. Dad's affair. My Mom used to talk to me every morning about Dad's affair and how hard it was on her. I am sure she didn't realize that what she was doing was detrimental to me.

8. Being date raped. I couldn't tell anyone because I thought it was my own fault.

9. My brother's death.

10. Dad's death two years later.

11. My sister-in-law, niece and nephew moving to Ontario and leaving me devastated.

12. My Mom's constant expectations – I was always too loud, too heavy; I either did too much or not enough. I never felt like I measured up to her standards.

13. I felt responsible for a friend's death even though I couldn't have prevented it.

14. Broken friendships.

15. The abortion of a ministry opportunity.

I could go on but that gives you a pretty good idea that my safety deposit boxes ran the gamut. Rejection, hurt, grief, fear, anger, guilt, sorrow, confusion, disappointment; they covered it all. I didn't realize how much "stuff" I had hidden away. When I came to fully understand the amount of "stuff" my safety deposit boxes held, I was devastated and I felt quite hopeless and unable to deal with it all. Thank God, literally, for my counsellor and my husband!

The interesting thing I discovered in this process was that I really was willing for God to be my All-Sufficient One. I had read a book called "Made to Crave" by Lysa TerKeurst, and in there she alluded to the fact that God wants us to find our sufficiency in Him. I found that I was able to do that during that time.

As I let Him take me through the traumas, disappointments and hurts that were stored in the "safety deposit boxes" I realized that I wasn't handing Him just the memories but all the fear, anger, sorrow, regret, guilt, and any other emotions that were attached to those memories. I finally let God deal with the memories and emotions and in return He gave memories and wholeness! Wow! What a trade-off! I gave Him all my uglies and He gave me back golden treasures.

It took me crying out Psalm 18:1-3 for the Lord to be able to answer my cry for healing. Psalm 18:1-3 reads: *I will love You, O Lord, my strength. The Lord is my rock and my fortress and my deliverer; My God my strength, in whom I will trust; My shield and the horn of my salvation, my stronghold. I will call upon the Lord, Who is worthy to be praised; So shall I be saved from my enemies.*

I am still learning to walk in that wholeness, but I have to say I felt like I lost 50 pounds in one week.

The Lord gave me what is talked about in Isaiah 61:1-3. The Spirit of the Lord God was upon me, because for this time He anointed me to basically preach to myself good tidings. He healed my broken heartedness and He set *this* captive free.

He opened the door of my "bank vault" and took all those memories and emotions that I hadn't dealt with that had me bound. I knew that this was His acceptable time He comforted me, gave me beauty for ashes, and the oil of joy for mourning and He gave me a garment of praise in exchange for the spirit of heaviness.

Off the Anti-Depressants
I Go

Chapter Four

So, thankfully, this much had been accomplished while I was still on the anti-depressants; but God wasn't finished yet!

As I mentioned earlier, February 4th was the day things got even more interesting, because this was the day when I started coming off the anti-depressants. I don't know if you have ever tried coming off anti-depressants, but let me tell you it is not a fun journey. I had tried several times before to come off the anti-depressants slowly and had crashed and burned every time.

So the thought of coming off them quickly, almost to the point of cold-turkey, scared me spitless. However, I understood why I needed to do this. It was to enable me to go on a different type of anti-depressant. So reluctantly I started the process of coming off both anti-depressants in ten days. I went off the Effexor immediately but weaned off the Wellbutrin over a ten day period. (Remember, this was so I could start a different medication.)

The first Sunday of this journey I was sitting in church, quite shaky and nervous, when my Pastor decided, led of the Holy Spirit I'm sure, not to preach the sermon he had prepared. Instead he asked us to share how we experienced God speaking to us. Several people shared and then he suggested that we have a quiet time and just wait for the Lord to speak to us individually. God came through big time!

As I was waiting I heard God speak to me in that small still voice: "My daughter, you do not go through this alone. I will uphold you with My righteous right hand. Will you leave your self-sufficiency at My alter and trust in Me? Then stand amazed, My daughter, at what the Lord your God will do for you". As you may well imagine, I cried buckets but that word holds me firm to this day.

Oh, how I needed those words of encouragement in the next week or two! Almost immediately as I came off the medications my emotions were all over the map. At times I cried so hard that I almost made myself sick. I was nauseated and had horrendous headaches but I held on to the promise of my God.

The best way I can describe what it felt like is to say that it felt like I had a tornado, a tsunami and a whirlwind going on inside of me all at the same time. I really had no clue how to deal with what was happening. I did know that I couldn't/didn't want to deal with things in my own self-sufficiency. The pain felt like it was going to tear me apart or overwhelm me but God's Word promised, and still promises that when I pass through the waters He will be with me.

Though we will walk together through the rivers, they will never overflow over me. When I walk through the fire, I will not be burned, nor shall the flame scorch me. For He is the Lord my God, the Holy One of Israel, my Savior (Isaiah 43:2-3 – personalized). And oh, by the way, He is true to His Word!

Pain Equals Longing

Chapter Five

February 14th - During my counselling session that week, my counsellor explained to me that every pain has a correlating longing attached to it. She suggested that I try to name the pain that I was feeling and then try to discern what the longing was that was attached to it. Then I was to pray and invite the Lord to validate and fill my longings. Apparently the intensity of the pain is comparable to the intensity of the longing. My pain/longing graph looked something like this:

Pain	Longings
Overlooked	To Be Validated
Unloved/Unwanted	To Be Loved/Cherished
Hopelessness	To Be Hope-filled
Feeling Unsafe	To Be Safe/Secure
Insignificance	To Be Significant
Outcast	To Belong

This was very beneficial for me, because I am a visual learner and I could definitely see how the pain and the longings correlated. I never realized that I had such deep longings tucked away in the recesses of my heart; yet God could and did satisfy each one. He continues to do so to this day, when I let Him. Just for clarification, a longing is any spoken or unspoken expectation that hasn't been met.

Psalm 107:8-9 in the Amplified Bible reads: *Oh, that men would give thanks to the Lord for His goodness, and for His wonderful works to the children of men! For He satisfies the longing soul, and fills the hungry soul with goodness.*

I am so thankful…

A Bold Decision Made

Chapter Six

Three weeks into counselling, and one week into coming off anti-depressants (in order to go on another anti-depressant), I felt the Lord tell me that I should go off the anti-depressants completely. Wow! Can you say scared?

However, I called my doctor and discussed it with him. I told him that I felt that this was of the Lord, but I also promised that if I felt I needed to I would use the prescription that he had given me. I assured him that my husband was at home and that he was aware of what I was doing and that he knew what to look for and that he would be a safe-guard for me. My doctor reluctantly agreed to let me try going off completely. That was six months ago and I am still going strong.

The Journey Continues – Journal Excerpts

Chapter Seven

From this point on I am including numerous excerpts from my journal. I hope this helps convey the rest of my story. I want to show that this walk into healing is not a once and done thing. Over the last 5-6 months I have run the gamut of emotions from despair of ever being truly whole to thanksgiving for where God has brought me. I swing back and forth between those dichotomies on a regular basis. I am a "journaller" so I thought I would give you insight into my journey by sharing my journal entries.

February 17/15

Genesis 25:11b (Amp) — *And Isaac dwelt at Beer-lahoi-roi [A well to the Living One who sees me].*

What does that mean for me? It means that I need to constantly live knowing there is a God Who sees me and desires to be my constant supplier of everything I need. When I dwell by the well of Lahoi-roi I *always* have an abundant and constant supply of everything I need: validation, and feelings of being loved and cherished, hopefulness and significance.

February 19/15

Yesterday I came to the understanding that depression actually "says" to a person: "Here, let me take that for you and together we can just stuff, repress and depress all those emotions surrounding that issue". So I decided to let Depression know that I didn't need it's help anymore and that God and I were going to be looking after things from here on out.

This is what I wrote in my journal: "So...Depression, I address you and tell you that I **do not** need your help in dealing with emotions that are attached to specific events is my life. I can say this because my All-Sufficient God will take care of things for me from this point on, and that includes any and all events and emotions from my past. 2 Timothy 1:7 states (personalized): For God has *not* given me a spirit of fear – but of power and of love and of a sound mind!! There is no memory or emotion that can come against me this day or in the days to come that my all-sufficient God and I can't handle together. So there!"

Another thing my counsellor wanted me to look at was if there was any unfinished business left to deal with in regards to the rape and the molestation that had taken place in my life. She explained that these types of events had taken something away from me and that I needed to give back the lies that I had bought into and take back the things that these events had stolen from me.

Again, I did some journaling: "Well, today God and I are giving back the lies that you, my transgressors gave me and we are taking back those things that you stole from me.

1) I am giving back feelings of 'yuck' about myself and my sexuality and I am taking back feelings of cleanliness and innocence.

2) I am giving back the need to keep lies and secrets and taking back the ability to walk away from those lies and secrets and to tell the truth.

3) I am giving back the responsibility for your actions to you and I am taking back the reality that I am not, and never was, responsible for your actions.

4) I am giving back a sense of not being enough and I am taking back the reality that God has made me enough."

I must say that this felt like quite an intellectual process. It wasn't what I expected or imagined. I had to remember that lots of tears and a tremendous amount of pain had preceded this exercise.

February 20/15

Dear God, thank you for loving me just the way I am, but at the same time loving me so much that You won't leave me in a place of despair and defeat! I am being transformed from glory to glory and I will continue to be in this transformation until I am, at last, fully glorified with You.

Philippians 4:13 - *I can do all things through Christ who strengthens me.* This includes walking this journey of healing.

February 23/15

Psalm 34:4 (Barb's paraphrase): I sought the Lord and He answered me! He delivered me from **all** my fears. Not some of them, all of them!

February 25/15

It is about claiming my identity in Christ. In Isaiah 61 God is basically talking about living in the opposite spirit...good tidings to the poor; heal the broken-hearted; liberty to captives; release those who are bound. Console those who mourn. Give them beauty instead of ashes. Oil of joy instead of mourning and a garment of praise instead of a spirit of heaviness.

So...if I look back at the pain graph, I have been allowing God to give me feelings of validation instead of feeling overlooked; feelings of being loved and cherished instead of feeling unwanted and unloved. He is giving me a spirit of hope instead of hopelessness; a sense of safety and security instead of feeling unsafe and insecure; a sense of significance instead of a sense of insignificance **and** an overwhelming sense of belonging rather than feeling like an outcast. Wow, this is powerful stuff!

March 1/15

Song of Solomon 4:16a – *Awake, O north wind and come, O south.*

Bring the north wind of trouble which will wake me from my slumber or the south wind of comfort and joy; anything is better than the dead calm of indifference, which is what medicated depression is like. That's what this time has been about! I have said it before and I will say it again: I am **not** leaving this place until You have accomplished everything You desire! I have set my face as a flint, to follow hard after You. Don't let me stop now – It is only the beginning!

"Life need not be easy, to be joyful. Joy is **not** the absence of trouble but the presence of Christ."

- William Vander Hoven

March 4/15

Joshua 1:9 - *Have I not commanded you? Be strong and courageous, do not be afraid nor be dismayed, for the Lord your God is with you, wherever you go!*

Isaiah 40:15, 17 - *Behold, the nations are as a drop in a bucket, And are counted as the small dust on the scales; All nations before Him are as nothing, and they are counted by Him less than nothing and worthless.*

As I was reading this passage this morning it was like God was saying, "Barb, your trials and tribulations are as the nations which are as a drop in the bucket and are counted as the small dust on the scale. In your own sufficiency they are overwhelming and insurmountable. There is no point in even trying to come against them. BUT when the great I AM is your sufficiency they really are miniscule. None of them are even sufficient to burn. They are all counted by Me as less than nothing and worthless."

This was not said in any way to negate the effect the trials and tribulations have had on me, but to encourage me that in His sight they are as nothing and I don't have to carry them around anymore.

He finished my devotional time with Isaiah 40:28-31: - *Have you not known? Have you not heard? The everlasting God, the Lord, The Creator of the ends of the earth, Neither faints nor is weary, His understanding is unsearchable. He gives power to the weak, and to those who have no might He increases strength. Even the youths shall faint and be weary, and the young men shall utterly fall, But those who wait on the Lord shall renew their strength; They shall mount up with wings like eagles, They shall run and not be weary, They shall walk and not faint.* Amen!

March 7/15

Mark 4 - Parable of the Sower

Personal discontent is probably the most encroaching "thorn crop" that I deal with. Yes, sometimes there are worries, once in a blue moon a hunger for the deceitfulness of riches but the big one for me is personal discontent. Discontentment with my weight, energy, ministry opportunities...always thinking about tomorrow.

What about being content in *this* day? What about reveling in God in *this* day? What about putting aside unhealthy spoken and unspoken expectations of self in *this* day?

Wouldn't that allow the truth of God's Word, that He loves me, to grow and flourish and consequently bring forth a healthy abundance of good fruit?!?

March 9/15

Isaiah 43:15, 18-19 – *I am the Lord, your Holy One, The Creator of Israel, your King. Do not remember the former things, nor consider the things of old. Behold, I will do a new thing, now it shall spring forth; shall you not know it? I will even make a road in the wilderness and rivers in the desert.*

Boy, this is sure where I feel like I am right now. I am kind of at that place where I don't feel like I fit in my own skin anymore. I know from experience that it will eventually become more comfortable again - or maybe I don't want it to. Comfort might be highly over-rated when in contrast I could learn to live *wholly* in the moment with God. To heck with comfort!

I *do not* want to be comfortable if it means shutting down. I did that for a long time and I don't want to go there again. I want my comfort to come from knowing that God has got my back *no matter what*! Lord, please help me to walk this out.

March 10/15

Today in counselling we discussed the difference between comfortableness and contentment. I believe it is contentment I seek. I don't *need* to be comfortable but I *do need* to be content. In the Bible, Paul never talked about comfort but he sure talked a lot about being content. Philippians 4:11reads – *Not that I speak in regard to need, for I have learned in whatever state I am, **to be content**.* (Emphasis mine)

May I learn to be content – moment by moment; hour by hour; day by day. *Then* I will live in that peace that passes all understanding.

March 14/15

1 Corinthians 10:12 - *Therefore let him who thinks he stands take heed lest he fall.*

Yesterday's grace is not enough! God's grace is new every morning! Therefore, I must appropriate His grace and His all-sufficiency every day, or perhaps every hour. It is not as though I have to dig hard to obtain today's grace. It is just there, waiting for me to appropriate it. It is only in His grace and all-sufficiency that I can *truly* live, move and have my being.

Jude 24-25 (personalized): - *Now to Him who is able to keep me from stumbling, and to present me faultless before the presence of His glory with exceeding joy, To God my Savior, who alone is wise, be glory and majesty, dominion and power both now and forever.* Amen.

March 16/15

Psalm 19:13a – *Keep back Your servant also from presumptuous sins; let them not have dominion over me.*

Good checkpoint! It is so easy for me to run ahead and in so doing I can easily fall into the sin of presuming that *I* can do it; when, in fact I *cannot!* Anything I accomplish from this day forth must be accomplished by the power of the Holy Spirit! - Mandated by Him; inspired by Him; and brought to pass by Him; through me. I only want to exalt His Name. Let my life be His story lived out through me!

March 18/15

1 Peter 5:8-11 (personalized): – *Barb, be sober, be vigilant; because your adversary (or enemy) the devil walks about like a roaring lion, seeking whom he may devour. Resist him, steadfast in the faith...But may the God of all grace...perfect, establish, strengthen and settle you. To Him be the glory and the dominion forever and ever.* Amen.

As I stay steadfast, with my focus on Christ and what He has called me to, God will perfect, establish, strengthen and settle me. This is where I need to be – In Christ and focused on Christ.

Part of this standing fast and being focused is realizing, more and more, what it means to be a child of God!

Lord, please fill me with a spirit of adoption until perfect love casts out fear. Thank You.

March 30/15

1 Samuel 30:6b – *...But David strengthened himself in the Lord his God.*

When times get rough and I don't know how to carry on I **must** strengthen myself in the Lord my God! He is my all-sufficient One! He is the one who is always in control. It is God who knows the beginning from the end! He alone can strengthen me. I might think I can manage on my own, but think again sweet-cheeks. That is what got me on anti-depressants in the first place!

God is the only One who can truly strengthen me!!!

Lord, You have so touched my heart in these last months that even thinking about Your goodness makes me want to cry. I can hardly believe that I have never known You like this before.

It is as though I have met you for the first time – maybe this is so. Maybe the Lord I thought I served was merely a shadow of the reality of the One True God. I know it was in ignorance but, oh, so many long and lonely years trying to prove myself to You.

May my testing bring a sweet aroma to Your throne and may I never lose sight of the God I have come to know in these last months. May I ever be aware of Your deep love and compassion that have brought me forth to this newness of life!

March 31/15

Isaiah 53:5-6 (personalized): - *But He was wounded for **my** transgressions, He was bruised for **my** iniquities, the chastisement for **my** peace was upon Him, and by His stripes **I** am healed.*

What an awesome, thought-provoking time of year to be walking out my healing. It brings home, in a very personal way, how much Jesus loved me and how much He sacrificed for me.

I am overwhelmed and overcome!!

The love that I now know He has for me brings me to my knees – literally. Again, I am gaining so much clarity of God's desire for **me.**

Truly I am more than a conqueror through Christ who loves me and gave His life for me. I am now able to praise in the midst of the battle because I "get it".

April 2/15

"Some of your best traits and some of your finest work will grow out of the incredibly painful periods in your life."

- Charles Swindoll – The Finishing Touches[1]

I have commented for a long time that growth happens in the valley, not on the mountain tops. And I can attest to that once again. I don't think I have ever been in quite this low a valley before but I tell you what...the growth has been absolutely amazing! All honor and glory, praise and adoration to Jehovah-Jireh, my Provider, and my All-Sufficient One.

April 4/14

2 Corinthians 5:17, 21(NIV) - *Therefore, if anyone is in Christ, the new creation has come: the old has gone, the new is here. Because, God made Him who knew no sin to be sin for us, that in Him we might become the righteousness of God.*

This is a powerful truth and it leads me to live a life of thankfulness and gratitude. I don't have to strive to be anything other than what I am.

I already have the righteousness of God because Christ took my sin to the cross. It is not anything that I have done, but everything that Christ has done on my behalf.

April 8/15

Philippians 1:6 – Personalized - *Being confident of this very thing, that He who has begun a good work in me will complete it until the day of Jesus Christ.*

Do I believe that God began a good work in me? *YES!* Well then, I need to believe he will complete it until the day of Jesus Christ. He is not going to leave me half-baked!

Psalm 23:4 - ...I will fear no evil; for You are with me...

What have I to fear if the Holy Spirit is with me? Nothing! He is more than capable of guiding and directing me in the way that I should go. And if there are storms along the way I still have nothing to fear, for He **is with me.**

April 9/15

I have just come to the profound realization of just how much "Fear" has stolen from me; and I declare that he no longer gets to win! I am adamant about this. Fear has owned enough of my life. **No more!** God is greater than any fear that might try to come against me!

"The safest route to follow is Authenticity Avenue, walled on either side by Accountability and Vulnerability."

- Charles Swindoll – The Finishing Touch[2]

"How easy it is to talk ourselves out of our destiny because we don't understand the value of our purpose."

- Marcella Paulette – Fellow Writer

Lord, please help me to understand the value of my purpose. You have set me here for such a time as this. Don't let me blow it off because of fear.

April 17/15

I love the song by TobyMac called, "Beyond Me". The chorus goes: "You gave me the stars put them out of my reach. Called me to waters a little too deep. Oh, I've never been so aware of my need. You keep on makin' me see its way beyond me."[3]

I need to remember as I walk this journey that it is Your idea, not mine. The song just focuses on the fact of my dire need for you. Anything You call me to is going to be beyond me **but** You and I can do it together! As it is way beyond me it becomes all about You!

April 23/15

Romans 8:37 - *Yet in all these things we are more than conquerors through Him who loved us.*

I must bring my all to the foot of His all-sufficient Cross. I couldn't save myself, neither can I conquer my sins by myself. Jesus is the only One who makes me able to stand against my enemies. He is my all-sufficient One. It is through Him that I live and breathe and have my being!

April 26/17

1 Corinthians 11:24 - *...Do this in remembrance of Me.*

Every day I need to remember Christ and **all** that He has done for me. I stand amazed at His work throughout my life, but especially at what He has accomplished in the last 4 months or so. From the absolute, utter pits of despair to freedom unknown prior to this time. Freedom – knowing that He loves me, cares for me and wants to use me just the way I am.

FREEDOM

April 27/15

Isaiah 30:18 (Amp) - *And therefore the Lord [earnestly] waits [expecting, looking, and longing] to be gracious to you; and therefore He lifts Himself up, that He may have mercy on you and show loving-kindness to you. For the Lord is a God of justice. Blessed (happy, fortunate, to be envied) are all those who [earnestly] wait for Him, who expect and look and long for Him [for His victory, His favor, His love, His peace, His joy, and His matchless, unbroken companionship]!*

God waits for me to come to the end of my rope so that He can show forth His all-sufficiency!

Psalm 67:6b - *...God, even our own God, will bless us.*

Not only do I not avail myself of the blessings of God, sometimes I don't avail myself of God, period. He has promised to be for me and not against me so why is He so often my last resort?

I have to learn the divine skill of making God everything to me! I need never be in want because I have an awesome God who longs to bless me. I never have to be in fear because He is fearless. I never have to tremble or be dismayed because He is **always** with me. Everything I have need of He will supply...if I ask Him to!

Thank you, Lord, that You patiently remind me that I have You as my pilot on this journey of life and that my life is so much less stressful when I come to You, my All-Sufficient One.

April 29/15

1 Peter 5:7 (Amp) - *Casting the whole of your care [all your anxieties, all your worries, all your concerns, once and for all] on Him, For He cares for you affectionately and cares about you watchfully.*

Philippians 4:6-7 - *Be anxious for nothing, but in everything by prayer and supplication, with thanksgiving, let your requests be made known to God; and the peace of God, which surpasses all understanding, will guard your hearts and minds through Christ Jesus.*

Lord, I still find myself fussing a lot and feeling overwhelmed. How do I stay in the place of knowing You are my All-Sufficient One? I am learning just how much I need to grow in this area called trust.

April 30/15

2 Corinthians 1:9-10 - *Yes, we had the sentence of death in ourselves, that we should not trust in ourselves but in God who raises the dead, who delivered us from so great a death and does deliver us; in whom we trust that He will still deliver us.*

Delivered, does deliver, will still deliver. God is the only One who can deliver me from the miry clay of the pit! Others may help but they are incapable of fully delivering me. God and God alone is my Deliverer. He must be - otherwise I will just fall back into the pit from which I was just rescued.

You are faithful! You never give up on me! Only You are able to finish all that You have started in me.

May 2/15

Joshua 1:9 - *Do not be afraid; do not be discouraged, for the Lord your God will be with you wherever you go.*

"Courage is resistance to fear, mastery of fear, **not** absence of fear."

- Mark Twain

I can't believe how huge fear is in almost every area of my life. Fear of success, fear of failure, fear of being too much, and fear of not being enough. Fear, fear, fear!

God doesn't want me living in fear and angst. That is where a lot of the feelings of being overwhelmed come from. But, my soul, I have nothing to fear...God is for me, who can be against me?

May 3/15

Psalm 46:1 - *God is our refuge and strength, a very present help in trouble.*

God **is** – not God was or might be – God **is** a very present help in trouble.

Present – meaning right here, right now.

So, God is right here to give me help in whatever situation or circumstance I find myself! He will continue to be a present help unto eternity; but I must appropriate the promises of God in order for them to be effective in my life!

Lord, please help me to not only acknowledge Your great and mighty promises but help me to actually take You up on them. The more I trust Your promises in my life the closer I will be to You.

Romans 12:2 - *And do not be conformed to this world, but be transformed by the renewing of your mind, that you may prove what is that good and acceptable and perfect will of God.*

Having a transformed mind doesn't just give me a better mind, it gives me a new mind. It is a bit like metamorphosis; the grub doesn't become a better grub, it becomes a beautiful new butterfly.

That is what is happening as I go through this journey...

May 8/15

Just as I was getting ready to go to sleep tonight I was thinking about my book and how fear has been such a big part of my story. I saw a little girl coming out of a big black cave, but coming out into the light was very scary for her because she had spent years in the blackness of the cave. She wasn't sure what to expect in the light. She was taking very timid steps and her eyes were darting around looking to see if something or someone was going to pounce on her. She clearly wanted to come out but it was obvious that she was terrified at the same time.

I think this is a picture of me at this precise moment in time. It feels like it wouldn't take a lot to make me scurry back into the blackness of the cave where life is known.

However, that little girl and I will make this journey together with God. Out into the light, into the meadow, where it is sunny and warm.

May 10/15

Isaiah 40:31 – *But those who wait on the Lord shall renew their strength; they shall mount up with wings like eagles, they shall run and not be weary, they shall walk and not faint.*

I was never intended to fight life's battles alone. It is not my strength that causes me to soar, but God's. His strength sees me through every moment of every day. If I will let Him, He will see me through and He will refresh me in the process.

May 11/15

Nahum 1:3 – *...The Lord has His way in the whirlwind and in the storm....*

This verse is very relevant for me today as I revisit the storms of three months ago. I am attempting to write my story and I find that there are still remnants of those storms echoing in my life. It is good to be reminded that God is in the midst of the storms.

A thought that I took away from this verse was that the Lord allows the storms so that I will draw close to Him; yet He is in the storm drawing me near to Him. So even in the midst of the storm He is wooing me.

Matthew 28:20 – *...I am with you always...*

He will never leave me. He is constantly present, minute by minute, hour by hour, and day by day.

May 13/15

Psalm 30:5 – *...Weeping may endure for the night,* **but** *joy comes in the morning.* (Emphasis mine)

So it is with my journey at this time. There are still periods of mourning **but** joy always follows.

May 16/15

I am having a really hard time this morning! Tears were there as I woke up. I miss Sassy like stink. She seems to be the catalyst right now and I don't know why.

Then my devotional reading is Zephaniah 3:17 – *The Lord your God in your midst, the Mighty One, will save; He will rejoice over you with gladness, He will quiet you with His love, He will rejoice over you with singing.*

Lord, I guess I need quieting this morning. I have to say I don't like learning this new way of walking, where everything seems to be up close and personal. Please help me to grow in my trust of You, the Living God, who gives me richly all things to enjoy. Your grace never runs out, Your river of bounty is ever-flowing and the well-spring of Your love is constantly overflowing towards me.

May 23/15

Psalm 138:8 – *The Lord will perfect that which concerns me; Your mercy, O Lord, endures forever; do not forsake the works of Your hands.*

It is not me who needs to fulfill the purposes and plans of God. It is God who will fulfill them through me. They are God's purposes and plans I just need to be willing to let Him use me!

This is a really different way for me to think, never mind to act. I'm impressed that I "got it"! Now I just need to let this truth settle in my heart. It is God, not me, that does the work.

My confidence must be in God:

1) He started the good work in me.

2) He is the One that will bring it to its proper conclusion.

3) It must be God or it will be in vain.

May 26/15

Psalm 5:22 – *Cast your burden on the Lord, and He shall sustain you; He shall never permit the righteous to be moved.*

Why do I find it so hard to cast my burdens on the Lord? Is it because I feel I should be able to handle everything on my own? Even if I could handle everything on my own, why would I want to when I have someone right here, willing to help? It's not like I even have to admit my weakness to another human. God already knows my weaknesses and He is still willing to help. It doesn't get any safer than that!

May 27/15

2 Samuel 9:13 (NLT) — *And Mephibosheth, who was crippled in both feet, lived in Jerusalem and ate regularly at the king's table.*

David didn't shun Mephibosheth even though he was "marred" and should not have been welcome at the king's table.

It is the same for me today. I don't belong at the King of Kings' table and yet He spreads a feast before me. He does this even though I am broken and marred because He sees, in me, the reflection of Jesus. Wow! He takes me from my miserable brokenness and sets me at His table because He sees Jesus in me. Amazing Grace!

May 28/15

Romans 8: 30-31(Amp) – *And those whom He thus foreordained, He also called; and those whom He called, He also justified (acquitted, made righteous, putting them into right standing with Himself). And those whom He justified, He also glorified [raising them to a heavenly dignity and condition or state of being]. What then shall we say to [all] this? If God is for us, who [can be] against us? [Who can be our foe, if God is on our side?]*

God has done everything for me to ensure that I meet Him face to face in heaven. There is nothing I can add to His completed work; I need only to stand firm and claim it!

May 31/15

1 Thessalonians 4:17 – *Then we who are alive and remain shall be caught up together with them in the clouds to meet the Lord in the air. And thus we shall always be with the Lord.*

Come, Lord Jesus, Come! Is it wrong just to want to be with You? I am so weary of this life here on earth and I so look forward to being with You in glory. I am sorry, but this life kind of sucks! It is definitely better than the anti-depressants but it sure isn't a cake walk. I don't know what I thought would be different? I guess I thought I would inherently change. I thought life would be easier and lighter, somehow. I thought I would be more carefree; perhaps that will come with time.

I just 'heard' the Lord ask me: "Why would you think you would inherently change? You weren't light and carefree before the anti-depressants; you have always been more on the melancholic side. Why would you think that would change?"

I don't have a good answer for that; I just thought I would be different.

David was a man after God's own heart and he wasn't exempt from trials and tribulations so why should I expect to be any different?

Or, how about Jesus, He was the Son of God and yet He was afflicted? There is nothing that has come, or will come, against me that Jesus hasn't already faced. With my strong Deliverer at my side I can do anything through Christ, who strengthens and delivers me!

Psalm 103:3 – *...Who heals all your diseases...*

Jesus heals me most effectively from the disease of sin.

"We trust Him and sin dies; we love Him and grace lives; we wait for Him and grace is strengthened; we see Him as He is, and grace is perfected forever."

- Bible Gateway Devotion[4]

There is no *dis-ease* that the Lord my God cannot heal. He created me, He can heal me – It is as simple and as profound as that.

Lord, I come to You this morning and I ask that You would finish that good work which You started in me. I know I didn't expect the walking out part to be this hard, but You knew it would be and You hold me still. Thank you for Your grace and comfort.

June 1/15

Genesis 1:5 – *...So the evening and the morning were the first day.*

I had an interesting take away from this Scripture. Light and darkness in a continuum; joy and sorrow the same; ease and suffering; rest and labor; such is the circle of life. If I didn't have light I wouldn't know what darkness was. If I didn't have sorrow I wouldn't be able to understand and experience joy. If I didn't have labor, I wouldn't enjoy rest the same way.

I need Jesus in my life to give me focus. His is the same yesterday, today and forever. (Hebrews 13:8) Not only are His attributes the same day by day, they never change according to my circumstances. The only thing that needs to change about my circumstances is my attitude.

June 2/15

This quote from Charles Swindoll really impacted me this morning: "The longer I live, the more I realize the impact of attitude on life. Attitude, to me, is more important than facts. It is more important than the past, education, money, circumstances, than failures, than successes, than what other people think, say, or do. It is more important than appearance, giftedness, or skill. It will make or break a company...a church...a home. The remarkable thing is we have a choice every day regarding the attitude we will embrace that day. We cannot change our past...we cannot change the fact that people will act in a certain way. We cannot change the inevitable. The only thing we can do is play on the one string we have, and this is our attitude..."

- Charles Swindoll – The Finishing Touch[5]

June 3/15

Lord, You are called the Great Physician and in Matthew 9:12 You say that You came to be a physician to the sick. I don't feel sick Lord, but I feel unwell. You know my lack of energy and stamina and my inability to 'push through' and more. I know it wasn't in my best interests to 'push through' in the first place so I'm kind of okay with that, but the lack of energy and the seemingly overwhelming exhaustion plus the inability to sleep deeply are really getting me. Please help me Lord! I can go to the doctor but all he is going to want to do is put me on drugs, because he can't solve what my underlying issues are. Only You can! Would You please reveal to me what is going on? Help me to be open with myself and my counsellor so that this 'walking out' process can go forward. I feel like I am stuck in miry clay and I am just exhausted trying to walk out of it. Please set my feet upon a solid rock.

That sounds silly because you have already set my feet on Christ, the solid rock- and yet...

I know there is stuff going on because I am clenching my teeth like mad and I am agitated on the inside.

Thank You, Lord, for undertaking on my behalf.

2 Corinthians 10:4-5 – *For the weapons of your warfare are not carnal but mighty in God for pulling down strongholds, casting down arguments and every high thing that exalts itself against the knowledge of God, bringing every thought into captivity to the obedience of Christ...*

It is amazing the amount of negative stuff I believe about myself. I was talking to my sister this morning and I told her I felt like I kept hitting a brick wall. She told me to draw a brick wall on a piece of paper and then label the bricks with the negative stuff that I was feeling and hearing in my mind. So, I did that, and then we prayed over it, burned the piece of paper and flushed it down the toilet never to be seen again.

June 4/15

Breakthrough or breakdown – I'm not quite sure which. Yesterday was really messy; Emotions all over the countryside, periods of heart-wrenching tears and questioning of God and self. Today doesn't seem to be starting off any better. It's like I have this endless well-spring of tears rising up from my inner-most being.

My devotional book just flipped back three weeks and I didn't notice. The title of the reading was "Storms" and it finished with this quote from William Cowper: "God moves in a mysterious way His wonders to perform; He plants His feet upon the seas, and rides upon the storm."

So in the midst of whatever it is I'm going through, God is right here with me.

Nahum 1:9 – *What do you conspire against the Lord? He will make an utter end of it. Affliction will not rise up a second time.*

I feel like I have to address this Scripture to Satan..."Satan, you have **no** authority to try to bring this depression on me again! It has been dealt with at the Cross! By the blood of Christ I send you back to the pits of Hell. Your assignment against me is cancelled! In the Name and power of Jesus Christ! Amen."

Even though I had a major melt-down, my counsellor feels I am doing very well. I was able to stand firm against the lies of the enemy and to stand on God's promises.

June 5/15

Psalm 29:11 (NLT) – *The Lord gives His people strength. The Lord blesses them with peace.*

Thank You, Lord, for giving me the strength and the peace to deal with yesterday. I honor and magnify You for who You are...not just what You do for me. But I love that You know that I need Your strength and peace...my own just won't cut it.

Genesis 7:16b – *...and the Lord shut him in.*

I know what it meant for Noah to be shut in the ark by the Lord but what does that mean for me? Noah was shut in, meaning he was kept safe from the flood, set apart and no evil could touch him. Outside the ark all was in ruins, but inside all was rest and peace because God ordained it.

What is my ark, Lord? Do you shut me in somewhere?

Please shut me in, in Your presence Lord, wherever that may be; that I might know the rest and peace that comes from being 'shut in' by my Lord and Savior.

June 8/15

1 Chronicles 5:22 – *for many fell dead, because the war was God's...*

Any time I fight a spiritual battle I must remember that the war is God's. Therefore, I cannot, I repeat, cannot be defeated. There may be seeming setbacks but the battle is God's and He will prevail if I don't lose heart and give up.

If the war is of God the victory is SURE!

The tribes of Rueben, Gad and the half tribe of Manasseh did not neglect to put on their armor and go forth into battle. But they did not go forth in their own strength. In the midst of battle they were calling on the Name of the Lord and He delivered them and established them over the Hagarites!

My enemies are different but my God is not! I put on my armor, I go forth into battle against my enemy, all the while calling on the Name of the Lord and He **will** make me victorious. He is my sword and shield! He is my Strong Tower! He is the Defender of the weak! I will trust in Him!

June 9/15

Matthew 7:13-14 – *Enter by the narrow gate; for wide is the gate and broad is the way that leads to destruction, and there are many who go in by it. Because narrow is the gate and **difficult** is the way which leads to life, and there are few who find it.* (Emphasis mine)

Interesting, I had always caught the part about the narrow gate but I don't think that I ever remember reading that the way is difficult. I tend to skip over those bits that don't fit with my 'rose garden' type of Christianity.

The truth of the matter is that the road can be very hard and difficult, but I am promised that I will never walk it alone and that it will never be more than I can handle. I am also promised that it will always be worth the journey!

June 13/15

Exodus33:14 – *And He said, "My Presence will go with you, and I will give you rest."*

Jeremiah 31:25 (NIV) – *I will refresh the weary and satisfy the faint.*

Mark 6:31 – *And He said to them, "Come aside by yourselves to a deserted place and rest a while."*

Today's word is apparently rest. Rest from whatever it is that drives me. I can think of a few things that I could rest from.

Rest from trying to measure up. Rest from trying to keep everything locked inside. Rest from the emotional turmoil of the last few months.

JUST REST

June 17/15

Psalm 12:1 – *Help, Lord...*

Short, sweet and to the point! When I ask Him to help me it doesn't mean that I expect Him to do everything for me. It means that He will participate with me to see something accomplished. Sometimes I think it would be more to the point to just cry out "Help, Lord" rather than go into a long-winded prayer. "Help, Lord" pretty much covers it all without me adding too much of my own agenda to the mix.

His ways are probably better than mine anyway!

June 18/15

Psalm 32:8, 10 – *I will instruct you and teach you in the way you should go; I will guide you with My eye. ...But he who trusts in the Lord, mercy (love) shall surround him.*

Not only does God long to guide me but He also desires to surround me with love and mercy. As I am obedient to follow Him, love is my constant companion.

Lord, please make me more aware of Your great love for me.

June 21/15

Psalm 91:1 (Amp) – *He who dwells in the secret place of the Most High shall remain stable and fixed under the shadow of the Almighty [Whose power no foe can withstand].*

All of Psalm 91 is powerful but I love how the Amplified Bible puts verse 1. I can stand stable and fixed, that means immovable, against the wiles of the enemy. Good to know!

There have been a couple of instances lately where my standing has been pretty shaky. Why is it so much easier to believe the lies of the enemy than to believe God's truth?

I think it is because the enemy of my soul speaks to me directly; whereas, lots of the time, God's truth is revealed generally, through the Bible. Yet even when God speaks to me directly I often find it easier to believe Satan and his lies. I imagine that speaks to my self-worth more than anything.

June 24/15

James 1:2-4 – *My brethren, count it all joy when you fall into various trials, knowing that the testing of your faith produces patience. But let patience have its perfect work, that you may be perfect and complete, lacking nothing.*

So, these Scriptures were cause for a mini melt-down. I am just so frustrated with myself, with life and with God. I am not writing my book; I'm not doing my business course; I'm not doing 'stuff' around the house and yet I seem to be exhausted.

I am becoming more in touch with myself, I guess, and I can't say I'm thrilled about that either. I just want God to come in and make it all better!

Exodus 3:10-14 – *Come now, therefore, and I will send you to Pharaoh...And God said to Moses, "I AM WHO I AM." And He said, "Thus you shall say to the children of Israel, 'I AM has sent me to you.'"*

Moses is having a major melt-down and a severe identity crisis and God's answer to his

92

dilemma is to tell him that He is "I AM". Basically He was telling Moses whatever Moses' need was, that God had it covered.

For me, today, that looks like:

I am so weary – I AM your rest

I am frustrated – I AM your Deliverer

I am so weepy – I AM your Comforter

I need to remember that He is my All-Sufficient One.

HE is the Great I AM

June 25/15

Philippians 4:5-6 — *...The Lord is at hand. Be anxious for nothing...*

I have never read it this way before. It is usually verses 6-8 that are quoted; but if I go back to verse 5 it puts it all in context.

The Lord is at hand, **therefore,** be anxious for nothing.

The great I AM is at hand! The All-Sufficient One is at hand!

Hello, He is **not** a God far off — **He is near at hand!!!**

July 9/15

Luke 4:18-19 – *The Spirit of the Lord in upon Me, because He has anointed Me to preach the gospel to the poor; He has sent Me to heal the brokenhearted, to proclaim liberty to the captives and recovery of sight to the blind, to set at liberty those who are oppressed; To proclaim the acceptable year of the Lord.*

This has been my Scripture verse for as long as I can remember. Yet, I never realized that I would be better equipped to fulfill it if I allowed Jesus to minister to me first.

The Spirit of the Lord was upon Jesus so that He could fulfill all of that in me. He preached the gospel to me. He healed, and is healing, me when I am brokenhearted. He has proclaimed liberty to this captive and has opened my eyes that I may see. He has proclaimed that this is the acceptable year of the Lord, for me.

July 10/15

1 Corinthians 2:9 – *...Eye has not seen, nor ear heard, nor have entered into the heart of man the things which God has prepared for those who love Him.*

Regardless of anyone else's actions, I am marked with a destiny. God has a plan for me.

God longs to partner with me as I enter this new chapter in my life. I can overcome a lot of stuff by myself **but** He is the One who gives me the strength to be truly healed. Then I will be able to say, with Paul: 2 Corinthians 4:7-9 (personalized) - *But I have this treasure in an earthen vessel that the excellence of the power may be of God and not of me. I am hard-pressed on every side, yet **not** crushed; I am perplexed, but **not** in despair; persecuted, but **not** forsaken; struck down, but **not** destroyed.*

July 15/15

Luke 8:46, 48 – *But Jesus said, "Somebody touched Me, for I perceived power going out from Me." And He said to her, "Daughter, be of good cheer; your faith has made you well. Go in peace."*

Jesus wasn't dismissing the woman when He told her to "go in peace"; He was sending her off with a blessing. "Daughter, your faith has healed you! Go in peace." In other words, no more stress or turmoil; she was healed and she could now be at peace. Jesus also restored her socially when He called her 'daughter'. She was no longer an outcast.

The power that went forth from Jesus to heal the woman with the issue of blood had **no** effect on His power to raise Jairus' daughter from the dead. He has more than enough power to heal **all** who come to Him, including me!

July 20/15

Romans 12:2 – *And do not be conformed to this world, but be transformed by the renewing of your mind, that you may prove what is that good and acceptable and perfect will of God.*

God wants me to renew my mind and one of the best ways I can to that is to bring every thought captive under the power and authority of His truth.

2 Corinthians 10:4-5 – *For the weapons of our warfare are not carnal but mighty in God for pulling down strongholds, casting down arguments and every high thing that exalts itself against the knowledge of God, bringing every thought into captivity to the obedience of Christ...*

I can also renew my mind by laying aside anxiety. Philippians 4:6 tells me not to be anxious for anything but instead to pray about everything. I can do that! Or at least I can try to do that!

Now I am reminded that I can do all things through Christ who strengthens me. (Philippians 4:13)

Fear is the major thought hurdle that I am dealing with this morning, so:

"Lord, I come to You this morning and I ask that as I lay fear at the foot of Cross that You will, by the Holy Spirit, fill me with power, love, a sound mind and confidence. Then, Lord, please help me get back to work on this book; it is driving me crazy! Amen.

July 21/15

Proverbs 18:21 - *Death and life are in the power of the tongue...*

I have to watch the words that come out of my mouth and the words that play in my head. Words don't have to be spoken aloud to be powerful. Spoken words may seem to have more impact, but I find, time and time again, it is the negative thoughts (words) that pull me down.

Even now I am thinking about what needs to get done for the book and my mind boggles a bit. I hear: "It's too hard; what was I thinking; it's never going to amount to anything anyway."

Now then, I know those thoughts are not truth because: 2 Corinthians 2:19 states that in my weakness He is made strong and Acts 1:8 tells me that I will receive power when the Holy Spirit comes upon me.

So, I can choose to live by my negative thoughts which only lead to death, or I can choose to change my thoughts and actually accomplish something.

"When talking about yourself, speak words of hope, health, encouragement, life and purpose – they are God's truth for you."

- Stormie Omartian[6]

July 22/15

2 Corinthians 12:9 (NLT) – *...My grace is all you need. My power works best in weakness. So now I am glad to boast about my weaknesses, so that the power of Christ can work through me.*

Lord, I surrender all that I am to You today. I surrender my strengths and my weaknesses, and everything in between, so that You can do Your perfecting work in me. Thank You that Your grace is all I need in order for Your power to be at work in my life. Please help me to leave behind striving, and help me to find my rest in You. I acknowledge, this day, that You are the only One who can bring me to perfection (maturity, wholeness and completeness) in You. Please help me to walk in surrender. Amen.

July 24/15

Proverbs 13:4 (NLT) – *Lazy people want much but get little, but those who work hard will prosper.*

Lazy isn't about doing nothing – it is about doing the less taxing or challenging tasks. I can keep busy all day and never get around to the 'hard stuff' – like writing my book.

I always get the hard stuff done but wouldn't it be better to do it first, with a right heart attitude; rather than leaving things until they feel like a pressure cooker and my attitude stinks?

"Instead of perfection as our goal, the end-point of our plans, what if we make Jesus our end goal?"

- Amy Carroll – Proverbs 31 Ministry[7]

July 27/15

I just discovered a cool distinction: 1Peter 5:8 says,... *your adversary the devil walks about like a roaring lion...*; while Revelation 5:5 states that Jesus *is* the Lion of the Tribe of Judah.

Satan just wants to pretend and make us believe that he has all power and authority; but in reality Jesus doesn't have to pretend because He **is** all power and authority.

Who am I going to believe? Satan or Jesus? My money is on Jesus!

July 29/15

Isaiah 55:11 – *So shall My word be that goes forth from My mouth; it shall not return to Me void, but it shall accomplish what I please, and it shall prosper in the thing for which I sent it.*

God promises that His word always accomplishes what He intends it to. I need this reminder as I get down to the hard business of writing the book. I need to remember that God is the One who makes me brave. I'm reminded of parts of a song by Amanda Cooke called, "You Make Me Brave". "You make me brave...You call me out beyond the shore into the waves...No fear can hinder now that love has made a way...You make me brave...No fear can hinder now the promises You made."

- Amanda Cooke[8]

They might be Amanda's words, but they are my heart's cry!

July 30/15

Any desire, not satisfied in Christ, will separate me from Him and cause me to be shattered! That's what happens when I try to be in control. It is my desire for answers my way and that is a good part of what led to the depression years. I thought that I was surrendered to God but I didn't let go of my need for control. I would not allow God to satisfy that particular need.

James 1:14-15 – *But each one is tempted when he is drawn away by his own desires and enticed. Then, when desire has conceived, it gives birth to sin; and sin, when it is full-grown, brings forth death.*

Wow! I never realized the impact that wanting control would have on my life. I didn't realize that the desire for control would lead me down such a dark path – one that would lead to death...and depression is death.

July 31/15

1 John 4:19 – *We love Him because He first loved us.*

It is not about how much I love God! It is about how much God loves me!! I had done absolutely nothing when Jesus came and found me. He came into my life because He loved me. So why have I made my Christian walk about how much I love Him?

I couldn't earn His love in the past,

It just was.

I can't earn His love in the present,

It just is.

I will never be able to earn His love in the future,

It will just always be!

August 3/15

John 15:2 – *Every branch in Me that does not bear fruit He takes away; and every branch that bears fruit He prunes, that it may bear more fruit.*

I never thought of coming off anti-depressants as a time of pruning but it could certainly be classified as one! I can name at least one unhealthy branch that needed to be pruned back before it sucked my very life-blood dry. That branch would be pride, with off-shoots of self-sufficiency.

In this pruning process God has been disciplining me so that I can be more and more like Jesus.

August 6/15

Psalm 16:11b – *...In Your presence is fullness of joy; at Your right hand are pleasures forevermore.*

Joy is not dependent on circumstances; it is dependent on being in God's presence. Joy is about inner contentment and understanding my purpose in life.

In his book "Think, Act, Be Like Jesus", Randy Frasee states: "The joy of Christ can replace or reduce stress." He goes on to say, "Joy becomes a filter through which we view life. Joy changes our perspective and perception. Joy allows us to adopt an eternal mind-set. Joy is an ongoing reminder that God is in control – that He is in charge of the outcome."[9]

I couldn't say it any better!

August 9/15

Mark 9:23 – *Jesus said to him, "If you can believe, all things are possible to him who believes."*

It is possible for me to live where fear and doubt quickly pass through my thoughts; with no lingering allowed. I need to arise to my position as a child of the King. It doesn't help anyone when I live in less than my full potential.

August 12/15

2 Timothy 1:7 – *For God has not given us a spirit of fear, but of power and of love and of a sound mind.*

If God has not given me a spirit of fear then it must come from Satan. I don't have to accept anything that he offers!

"Satan, I address you right now and I tell you that I will not listen to your fear-mongering anymore! **God has given me a spirit of power, of love and of a sound mind** and fear **cannot** stand against it."

Lord, when I am feeling weak, tired and overwhelmed (like I am today) please open my eyes that I might see You, my Strong Deliverer. Please help me to lean on and rely on You and Your all-sufficiency. I worship You, God – there is none like You. Amen.

August 17/15

Barb, "you don't have to try to be someone you are not. I love you just the way you were created. Don't compare yourself to anyone else. I have given you unique gifts and talents, and I have called your for such a time as this. If you allow frustration to flood your heart, you only hinder My Grace. So reject comparisons. Reject frustrations. Reject striving. Embrace who you are now! Move forward as the person I have called you to be and your unique gifts will make room for you."

- Excerpted from Mornings With Holy Spirit, Jennifer LeClaire[10]

"Lord, thank you for Your words of encouragement and for helping me on this journey. Please help me to embrace myself and all that You have put within me."

August 23/15

"Woe is me, Lord, I am undone!!! I don't know how to do this. I feel like everything is closing in on me again. Everything, in this particular case, is all about the book. I don't know how I'm supposed to finish it; I don't know how to get testimonials when it isn't even finished yet...**I DON'T KNOW!!!!**

Lord, YOU KNOW! Please help me! Thank You, that in the midst of my overwhelmedness You are my peace. In the midst of my sorrow, You are my comfort. In the midst of my fatigue, You are my rest.

It's hard, because while I am trying to get this book done, life is still happening. HELP!!!

August 26/15

2 Corinthians 1:20-22 – *For all the promises of God in Him are Yes, and in Him Amen, to the glory of God through us. Now He who establishes us with you in Christ and has anointed us is God, who also has sealed us and given us the Spirit in our hearts as a guarantee.*

All the promises of God are fulfilled in Christ and they are YES and SO BE IT! I am taking this to mean that there is a breakthrough for complete healing and wholeness. **YES and AMEN!**

August 27/15

Numbers 21:17 – *Then Israel sang this song: "Spring up, O well! All of you sing to it..."*

I am singing to the well of living water that is bubbling within me right now –

"I've got a river of life flowing out of me! Makes the lame to walk and the blind to see! Opens prison doors, sets the captives free! I've got a river of life flowing out of me.

Spring up, o well, within my soul!

Spring up, o well, and make me whole!

Spring up, o well, and give to me

That life abundantly."

-L. Casebolt, HigherPraise.com[11]

God promised the people water but they needed to believe for it and that is why they sang. *As they sang the water sprang forth.* The water didn't come until they started to sing and then as the water bubbled forth, their song was even more joyous.

"Let it be so in my life, Lord, let it be so." And He said, "Yes and Amen!!!"

Deeper Revelation

Chapter Eight

This has been percolating for me since the beginning of June when I attended a Ladies Retreat.

Ezekiel 37:1-15. I am not going to write all of this Scripture out but it has to do with Ezekiel in the Valley of Dry Bones and God asking him if the dry bones could live. Ezekiel's answer was: "O Lord God, You know." (Verse 3)

Then the Lord commands Ezekiel to speak to the dry bones...Long story short Ezekiel speaks to the bones, they are covered with muscle, sinew and flesh and they turn into a mighty army.

The speaker challenged us that night to speak to the 'dry bones' in our own lives and watch God bring life and wholeness to areas that were dead and dry. I wasn't really willing to do that at that time, so things percolated.

In July I read a quote from Dr Dan B. Allender that really impacted me and made me think. Dr Allender states that he believes that: "The first great enemy to lasting change is the propensity to turn our eyes away from the wound and pretend things are fine. The work of restoration cannot begin until a problem is fully faced."[12]

Wow! That is a powerful statement and it got me thinking that maybe there was some hard work that I still needed to do but I still wasn't willing to work on it yet.

Finally, this past week, the Lord revealed to me that when I first came off the anti-depressants I acknowledged there were a lot of hurts in my safety deposit boxes, I had asked Him to heal them but I had never acknowledged the damaging effects of the contents of those boxes. These are my 'dry bones'.

So, the time has come to delve deeper into those safety deposit boxes. The questions I need to ask, as I do that, are:

1) How did this event really impact me?

2) What part of me died that needs the breath of God on it?

Once I have answered those questions I need to apply the truth of God's Word to those particular issues. In other words, I need to ask God to breathe life into those areas.

Here goes! The first box I need to look at is when Mom and Dad didn't want me when they found out Mom was pregnant. This put to death my sense of self-worth and belonging. I have spent my entire life trying to be good enough so that people will love me and accept me and this has often kept me from being true to myself and God. God's truth: I am fearfully and wonderfully made and all my days were written in His book before I ever was. His thoughts towards me have always been precious and I could never count them. (Psalm 139:14-18).

Second box – being pushed down the stairs by my babysitter. Again this attacked my sense of worth and being 'good enough'. It left me with a sense of being a bother so I tried to make myself invisible and to not rock the boat. I need my sense of self to be revived. God's truth: He has loved me with an everlasting love. He chose me before the foundation of the earth. When God made me He saw that I was good. (Jeremiah 31:3; Ephesians 1:4; Genesis 1:31).

Boxes three and eight– being molested by my babysitter and being date raped when I was twenty. These events stole my innocence, left me feeling 'dirty', and again left me feeling less than; because if I had been valuable to either of them they never would have hurt me. God's truth: I am more valuable to Him than the birds of the air...And He looks after them very well! He will never leave me; He is my helper and I will not fear. (Matthew 6:26; Hebrews 13:5-6).

Fourth box – being left home from holidays because I was sick. Even though this was by my own choice it still left me feeling abandoned, forsaken, unimportant, and not of any value. God's truth: again I am reminded that He loves me with an everlasting love; that He will not forget me and that He has me inscribed on the palms of His hands. (Jeremiah 31:3; Isaiah 49:15-16).

Fifth box – Daddy breaking a promise to me after I broke my leg. This left me feeling that other people were more important than me and that promises were made to be broken. God's truth: He will never leave me nor forsake me. In Christ, all the promises of God are yes and amen. (2 Corinthians 1:20; Hebrews 13:5).

Sixth and seventh boxes – Moving to Vancouver when I was 12 and leaving all my friends behind. This left me feeling lost and very insecure. That the same time, my mom and dad were going though marriage difficulties and I felt very caught in the middle. As an aside, if you ever have marriage difficulties please, please don't put your kids in the middle. I don't think my mom realized what she was doing but it was devastating for me.

I became a keeper of secrets because I couldn't tell anyone about what was going on at home and that left me feeling very isolated. God's truth: He will strengthen me, help me, and hold me in His righteous right hand. I can cast all my anxieties on Him because He cares for me. He will walk with me through the hard places; His rod and staff comfort me. I can be strong and courageous for it is the Lord that goes with me. He will never leave me nor forsake me. Nothing can separate me from the love of God. My help will always come from the Lord. I have a friend who sticks closer than a brother. (Isaiah 41:10; 1Peter5:7; Psalm 23:4; Deuteronomy 31:6; Romans 8:35-39; Psalm 121:1-2 and Proverbs 18:24)

Boxes nine, ten and eleven –These boxes have to do with my brother and dad dying within two years of each other and my sister-in-law moving back to Ontario after that with my niece and nephew. Total devastation is what comes to mind. The heart-numbing pain of 'losing' five close family members in the space of two years left me barely functional. Yes, I still had my mom and my sister but I was only able to focus on what I had lost. My will to live hit a low spot at this time of my life and it was all I could do to go on. I felt totally forsaken. God's truth: I will never be forsaken by the One who loves me most. I can do all things through Christ who strengthens me, including moving on from these heart-wrenching memories. (Deuteronomy 31:8; Joshua 1:5; Isaiah 62:12 and Philippians 4:13).

Box twelve – This one is a biggie for me. I always felt, that as far as Mom was concerned, that I never measured up to her standards. It seemed like I was always too loud or too quiet; I either did too much or not enough and I always weighed too much...this one was never too little. I felt, and sometimes still feel, manipulated by her even though she is gone. I still hear her voice in my head telling me all the things I am not. **But** God's truth: I am fearfully and wonderfully made and I was skillfully and intricately formed. God's thoughts toward me are precious and are so numerous that they can't be counted. God will always be for me. (Psalm 139:14-18; Romans 8:31).

Box thirteen – I have felt responsible for a friend's death even though I couldn't have prevented it. This has left me with a weight of guilt that is not mine to carry. God's truth: I can come to Him with my heavy burdens and He will give me rest. He also knew the number of my friend's days and there was nothing I could have done to change that. (Matthew 11:28; Psalm 39:4)

Box fourteen – Broken friendships. Again I am left with feelings of insecurity and vulnerability. I have taken responsibility for my part in the breakdowns but there is still an empty void where those friendships used to be. God's truth: He is one that sticks closer than a brother. He knows my need for relationships. (Proverbs 18:24; Genesis 2:18)

Box fifteen – The abortion of a ministry opportunity. I was involved in a ministry that I felt was to go across Canada but it did not transpire the way I believed it would, and the ministry died. This left me confused, hurt and wondering if I had heard from God. God's truth: He knows the plans He has for me are for good and not for evil, to give me a hope and a future. I also know that my ways are before the Lord and He ponders all of them. (Jeremiah 29:11; Proverbs 5:21)

Dear Lord,

As I have examined the contents of these safety deposit boxes and recognized the impact that they have had on me I ask that You would breathe life on all the 'dry bones' in my life that have been left for dead. Please bring newness of life to every area that has been compromised that I might arise as a mighty army. I want to be whole so that I can bring wholeness to others.

Amen

It is important to now seal up the 'bank vault' and the safety deposit boxes within it so that I don't ever try to use them again.

Lord,

Please take my bank vault and the safety deposit boxes that are within it and seal it up for eternity. I don't want to go back to using it; I want to go forward trusting You to look after any issues that come out from here on out.

Please help me to be aware of when I'm trying to fall back into that and snip that behaviour in the bud. I declare that You are my All–Sufficient God from here on.

August 28/15

1 Peter 2:9 (Personalized) — I am part of a chosen generation, a royal priesthood, a holy nation, His own special daughter, that I may proclaim the praises of Him who called me out of the darkness and into His marvelous light!!

I have obtained mercy!

Boy, did I ever need this after my soul searching yesterday. I have to say, I don't feel much like a part of a royal priesthood but I will cling to the truth that I am His special daughter. In spite of my messes, actually more accurately, because of my messes, He sought me out and to this day He loves me with an everlasting love.

Oh, how I need to cling to that truth!

Day by Day

Chapter Nine

I don't want to leave you with the impression that this is the end of healing for me. I know that I will be on this journey of wholeness until the day I die, or Jesus returns, which ever happens first. However, my story for this, time needs to end here.

I hope that reading my journal entries has been of help to you. The next section focuses on advice for individuals, and their loved ones, that suffer from depression.

Part Two

Strategies and Guidelines

INTRODUCTION

In this second part I would like to lay forth some guidelines that will hopefully assist you in walking out of the shadows of whatever your particular vault might be. This is by no means a comprehensive how-to list, merely some thoughts to head you in the right direction.

Before I go any further I want to categorically state that being on anti-depressants does **not** make you 'lesser than'! I trust these guidelines will help you whether you come off anti-depressants or not. Hopefully they will be some tools that you can use to get more out of life...anti-depressants or not!

First Things First

Chapter One

May I strongly suggest, if you have not already done so, that you accept Jesus Christ, the Son of God, as your personal Lord and Savior? The relationship that He longs to have with you will give you personal help from a personal God on what I anticipate could be an arduous journey.

I am a very strong person, but I know that I could not have walked this journey in my own strength. Even with my relationship with Jesus this has not been an easy journey for me but at least I know that I have a champion who will help carry me through.

Any number of my journal entries show where Jesus has come alongside of me and carried me through. For instance, on February 8th He spoke to my heart and told me that I do not go through this journey alone. He encouraged me that He would uphold me with His righteous right hand, that He would see me through, and that I would be amazed at what He would do on my behalf. Needless to say this has been instrumental in seeing me through the rough times.

I know He will see you through your journey in a very similar way. He promises to be a very present help in time of trouble. (Psalm 46:1).

If you have never accepted Jesus as your Lord and Savior it is as easy as ABC.

A – Admit that sin has separated you from God and you need Him, Jesus, to reconcile or make you right with God.

B – Believe that He is the Son of God and that He died for your sins; that He was buried and rose again on the third day and that He sits at the right hand of God praying for each and every one of us.

C – Confess your sins to Him and receive His forgiveness and His gift of eternal life.

A prayer might go something like this:

Jesus, I admit that my sins have separated me from God. I believe that You are the Son of God and that You died for my sin that I might be in right relationship with God. I believe that You were crucified, buried and that You rose again on the third day. I also believe You now sit at the right hand of God and that You pray for me. I confess my sins; I repent of them and ask that You would forgive me and enable me to have a right relationship with God. Amen.

Now hold on tight because you are going to go on the journey of your life.

(If you have prayed this prayer for the first time or would like to follow up on what this means for you, please feel free to contact me.)

Choose Life Not Death

Chapter Two

As I mentioned in my story, I had merely chosen survival for a long time. While you might not think of survival as death, it certainly isn't living.

When I think of survival now, it reminds of me of the Zombies that are so popular in today's culture. Zombies are the living dead and for me that was what depression was like. I was alive but I sure didn't feel like I was living. Can you relate?

It doesn't matter whether your shadows are from depression or something else. What does matter is that they are causing you to exist like a Zombie. One of the living dead!

Even before I embarked on this aspect of my journey He had led and guided me. When I was 12 years old we had just moved out to

Vancouver and I very seriously contemplated suicide. However, Jesus showed me that the Capilano Dam really wasn't that high and that I would just end up living, what I perceived to be a very hard life, in a broken body. I made the choice that day not to commit suicide. Life not death!

In 1997 I hit another really hard patch. My mom and I were very co-dependent at the time and she had totally misunderstood something I had said and had moved as far away from me as she could while still living in Calgary. I was already on anti-depressants but I didn't know how to handle the ensuing emotions. Rather than deal with them I seriously contemplated suicide again. I had it all planned and it would have worked but that 'still small voice' directed me to call a friend and ask for help. I chose life, not death.

Choosing life is the best decision I have ever made. Has it been easy? Not on your life! But I wouldn't go back to survival mode even if you paid me a million dollars. (I might contemplate it for a million dollars, but I know that life would win. What good would a million dollars be if I was merely surviving?)

So, you have a choice to make. You can show up and live life with all of its ups and downs or you can sit on the side-lines letting life pass you by, like a Zombie.

You have a choice!

Feel Your Feelings

Chapter Three

One of the major changes you are going to have to make when you choose life, is that you will need to start to own your feelings.

Eww! "Feelings", you say? "I don't do feelings!" Trust me; you will start to do feelings. There will probably be a whole slew of emotions that you never even knew you had. At least that is how it was for me.

Sadness I could understand. There had been a lot of rough things happen over the course of my life, but I was unprepared for the **overwhelming** sense of sadness. I literally felt as though my heart had broken- I mean shattered! Wow, I didn't expect that, but I got it.

What really took me by surprise was the anger. I had no idea that I had so much anger bottled up inside of me. I have heard it stated that anger is hurt turned inwards and for me that appears to be truth. Hurt is an acceptable emotion but what do you do with anger, which doesn't seem to be quite as acceptable?

As anger started coming to the fore bit by bit, I had to ask the Lord to help me to deal with it. He took me through the safety deposit boxes that I thought dealt with hurt and showed me how much of it was actually anger. Both emotions are similar, in that in order to deal with either of them, I had to be willing to forgive.

This was a process for me. I know that in some areas the Lord asked me to forgive the person, and just like that, it was done. In other areas I have had to work at it. I have had to give up my 'right' to revenge and recognize that the person involved probably didn't even mean to hurt me. They were probably acting out of their own woundedness. When I can 'get me out of the way' it is easier to see the other person's actions for what they truly were.

For instance, let's look at the incident when my baby sitter pushed me down the basement stairs. When I first opened that safety deposit box I thought it was hurt that I would be dealing with. Oh no, let me tell you, the emotion that rose up within me was raging anger. How could anyone treat a two and a half year old that way? Boy, if she'd been in the room I would have given her more than just a piece of my mind! However, once I had calmed down a bit the Lord showed me that she had been abused as a child. That was how she had been treated, so that was how she treated me. Once I got that, it was easier to forgive her. I'm not saying it was a snap to forgive her but it was easier.

How are your emotions doing? Any hurt, bitterness, anger or resentment that you have bottled up needs to be dealt with. Any wounds that need to be healed? Get your feelings or emotions out into the light of day and let the Light of the world show you how to deal with them. They **must** be dealt with, sooner or later, as otherwise they will just sit there and fester.

Remember, feelings and emotions are only a perception of reality. Once you have admitted your feelings and dealt with them, you are free to move on. You don't have to stay stuck in the pain, the anger, the hurt or the fear. You can release them and move on!

David felt emotions on a regular basis. Heck, just read a handful of the Psalms and you'll know what I'm talking about. **But**, after he acknowledged his emotions he chose to fix his eyes on God and to let God's truth become his reality.

Be Ready

Chapter Four

Before I ever got to the point of coming off the anti-depressants, God had been getting me ready.

On October 30, 2014, not too long before my mom died, the Lord awakened me from a sound sleep. I remember hearing Him gently calling my name. Our conversation went something like this:

God: "Barb, Barb."

Me: "Yes, Lord?" (I wasn't questioning that it was the Lord, I was questioning why He was calling me.)

God: "Last time I checked I was God and you were not."(He said this with a slight inflection of sarcasm.)

Me: "Oh yeah! I vaguely remember something about that."

God: "So, when are you going to give up control of your life to Me?"

Me: "Oh!"

That was the end of our conversation. I thought it had to do with the timing of Mom's death but it was about so much more than that. You see, I had committed my life to the Lord but I tried to keep control of it. This was God's gentle way of reminding me that it was His job to be in control of every area of my life, not mine. In little ways, and not so little ways, He started showing me that I could let go and let Him be in control.

It seemed like every time a decision had to be made He would remind me that it wasn't solely my decision to make. Once, I was talking to my husband about the possibility of leaving massage therapy. I had my lists of pros and cons and I even had some ideas as to what I might do instead. I had it all figured out; my husband didn't have to say a thing. Then I heard that small, still voice saying:

"Ahem, I am God and you are not." Well then, I had a choice. I could go ahead with my own plans or I could ask God what He had to say about the matter. Needless to say, I set aside my plans and followed His direction. FYI, I am still doing massage therapy. My desire to stop doing massage had more to do with me being tired than the fact that I really didn't want to do it anymore.

I have learned not to make decisions when I am tired.

Another way the Lord had been getting me ready was through a Bible study called "Made to Crave" by Lysa TerKeurst. Through doing the study I came to the understanding that God wanted me to find my sufficiency in Him, rather than in myself. That really struck a chord with me and I prayed and asked God to be my All-Sufficient One.

Little did I know what I had prayed – but God did! He took me at my word and started calling me to rely more and more on Him.

This was in January 2015, when I had already realized that the anti-depressants weren't working. By the time I came fully off them in February I was more than aware of how much I needed Him to be my All-Sufficient God.

One of the songs that really impacted me during this time was "Lord I'm Ready Now" by Plumb. One of the verses goes: "I've nothing left to hide, no reason left to lie; give me another chance; 'cause Lord I'm ready now"[13].

What about you? Can you think of any ways that God might be trying to get your attention? Any 'still, small voices' or loud big ones for that matter that are calling out to you? What about books you might have read that have struck a chord, or songs that have impacted your heart? Tune in and see what God has in store for you.

Ask The Hard Questions

Chapter Five

Don't be afraid to ask yourself the hard questions. I'm not talking about the 'whys' or the 'how comes'. I'm talking about the nitty gritty questions like the ones I asked near the end of my story. Those are the hard questions.

How did this event impact my life? What emotions were damaged? How was my authentic self compromised? What was my part, if any, in this event? What does God's truth say about this event?

Let's look at one of my boxes for an example. We'll look at being pushed down the stairs by my babysitter. This doesn't seem like a real biggie to me as an adult, but by virtue of the fact that this incident got put in a safety deposit box it shows me that there had to have been some damage done. That damage was more than I recognized. This event impacted me by making me feel 'less than', that I was a bother, that I never wanted to rock the boat and that I was better off if I was invisible. It also left me feeling very insecure and unwanted.

My authentic self had been created to be strong and courageous, confident and secure. I had also been created to be seen and heard; not to be silent and hidden away. Do you see what I'm getting at here?

I don't believe that I had a part in this particular incident except that I was there at the wrong time.

Now, we need to look at what God's truth says about the matter. His truth says: He has loved me with an everlasting love. He chose me before the foundation of the earth. When God made me He saw that I was good. He actually has commanded me to be strong and courageous. (Jeremiah 31:3; Ephesians 1:4; Genesis 1:31; Joshua 1:9).

Let's look at another box; maybe one that I have some accountability for. How about we look at the box of broken friendships? Now we all know it takes two to tango, and so it is when it comes to relationships.

The first thing I had to do with this box is to accept my own responsibility in the breakdown. Some of these friendships just died a natural death, some died partially due to neglect on my behalf, while others died because I hadn't dealt with my woundedness. I needed to take responsibility for the neglect and, as you know I'm still working on the areas of woundedness from other boxes. I did this by praying and asking for God's forgiveness where I had neglected and hurt others and I made amends with them as much as was welcome on their part. (This has been an ongoing process for some time now, not just since February.)

After I did that I was still faced with the questions of: "How did that affect me? What emotions were affected? And what are God's truths?"

As I stated earlier I was left with a sense of insecurity and vulnerability and I needed God to fill the empty void.

God forgave me for my part in the broken relationships and then He spoke to the insecurity and vulnerability. His truths are: I will never be left or forsaken by Him; I have a friend, Jesus, who sticks closer than a brother; and He knows my need for relationship.

So that is a bit of how you ask the hard questions. Are you ready? I suggest that you take some time alone and just go through your events as the Lord leads you to. Yes, it will be scary, but it will be well worth the journey.

Renew Your Mind
– Speak Truth

Chapter Six

It is so important, as you go through this journey, that you take the time to put God's truth into your mind. If you leave the same negative tapes playing, nothing will change even though you have done the hard work and asked the hard questions. This doesn't always come easily because we have a pattern to overcome.

There has been a significant change for me, even while I've been writing this book. Before, if I found things hard or if I didn't know how to do something I would just say, or often just think: "I can't do this." That was my fallback phrase…"I can't". Just as recently as a week ago, I was going through a mini melt-down and for the first time that I can remember, I didn't say, "I can't". Instead, I said, "I don't know how to do this...I don't know what I am supposed to be doing." Small change in words, big change in perspective!

That change came about because I had been putting God's truth into my mind and I had consciously been trying to watch the words that I spoke. The particular truth that relates to this episode is found in James 1:5, which states: *If any of you lacks wisdom, let him ask of God, who gives to all liberally and without reproach, and it will be given to him.*

I asked God for wisdom and discernment and He gave it to me. Yay, God!

Another example that comes to mind for me is a phrase that I used to use a lot, which was: "This is too hard!" God's truth says that I can do all things through Christ, who strengthens me. (Philippians 4:13).

So you see, God has truths for pretty much any negative thoughts or words that we might want to use. I am still in the process of replacing negative thoughts, words and actions with positive ones and God is more than faithful to help me is this project.

Some things that have helped me with this are:

1) Get into Scripture; find out what God says.

2) Ask friends to help keep me accountable.

3) Make sure I get enough rest; I am less negative when I look after myself.

4) Be a bit more discerning about what I read and what I watch on television.

5) Watch how I spend my free time; I do better if I make constructive use of my time rather than sitting on the computer.

So, are you ready to start renewing your mind? It is a challenge but it is well worth it! Your life will love you!

Expect Setbacks

Chapter Seven

I think this is self-explanatory. As in any journey of healing there are going to be setbacks. They happen. They are natural. Get over them and move on.

Having said that, could you please be gentle with yourself? When I say "get over them and move on", I don't mean brush off any stumbling blocks or regressive behaviour as though they shouldn't exist. What I do mean is don't let them bog you down until you are paralyzed.

Acknowledge the setback. Maybe ask some questions around it; such as: what triggered it, what else is going on, are you overtired, etc. Give yourself time to catch up with the growth that is happening and then continue to move forward into all that God has for you.

Walk Out Your Healing

Chapter Eight

By this I mean that you have to be willing to move forward in your healing, even though sometimes it might be hard.

Romans 14:7-8 – *For none of us lives to himself and no one dies to himself. For if we live, we live to the Lord; and if we die, we die to the Lord.*

The Lord could have taken us home in the nano-second that we were saved. Sometimes it seems that a righteous and loving God would do that; but then who would show His love, mercy and compassion to others? Who would show forth the amazing love of the Lord if we all went home to heaven as soon as we were saved?

No! We are still here so that we can bring glory to Christ in our daily lives and give others cause to recognize that God loves them too. We are to work together with God because it is His will that none should perish, but that all would come to a saving knowledge of His grace.

A prime example of this for me is writing this book. There have been many times in the last months when I really wished that God had taken me to heaven when He saved me. It has been a hard journey but if I can help one person learn that God is for them and not against them, then my job is done. I had a story to tell and I told it; the rest is up to God.

Another way I have walked out my healing is by sharing with people in my massage therapy practice. I just need to be obedient to do what He shows me to do.

How might you walk out your healing? Is there someone you can tell? Is there a story to be written; a song to be sung?

However it is that God shows you how to walk out your healing, please be faithful to do so.

We all need to hear testimonies of God's great faithfulness! It is others' testimonies that often give us the faith to believe for our own miracles.

One Day at a Time

Chapter Nine

In conclusion, let me encourage you to take this journey one day at a time. You may find that you have a lot of changes to go through, don't try to hurry the process. It is a process! You will not wake up one morning to find that you are perfectly whole and healed. If you allow God to take your hand and walk you through this journey you will notice changes over time. Rejoice in the seemingly small achievements because there are no small achievements with God.

Be blessed as you walk forward, knowing that every step toward healing is a step in the right direction!

Listen closely and you will hear the sound of clapping and cheering for every forward step you take.

Endnotes

[1] Charles R. Swindoll, *The Finishing Touch: Becoming God's Masterpiece.* (Dallas TX: Word Publishing, 1994), p. 173.

[2] Swindoll. 185.

[3] TobyMac, *Beyond Me.* © 2015 ForeFront Records, http://youtube.com/tobymacmusic

[4] BibleGateway Devotionals

[5] Swindoll.

[6] Stormie Omartian, FaithGateway Devotionals, July 21, 2015, www.faithgateway.com

[7] Amy Carroll, devotions @proverbs 31.org, July 24, 2015, http://proverbs31.org

[8] Amanda Cook, Bethel Music, *You Make Me Brave.* http://youtube.com

[9] Randy Frasee, FaithGateway Devotionals, August 06, 2015, www.faithgateway.com

[10] Jennifer, Le Claire, excerpted from Charisma Magazine – SpiritLed Woman, August 17, 2015, www.charismamag.com

[11] L. Casebolt, *I've Got a River of Life.* www.higherpraise.com/lyrics/cool/i/7194.htm

[12] Dr. Dan B. Allender, *The Wounded Heart.* (Colorado Springs, CO: NavPress, 2008), p. 14.

[13] Plumb, *Lord I'm Ready Now.* http://youtube.com

About The Author

Barb Tatlock is a woman who longs to bring healing to the broken-hearted. She has been a Massage Therapist for 25 years, bringing healing to the physical body. Barb now feels that the time has come to concentrate on helping others by facilitating transformational healing in the mental and emotional realms.

She speaks from a place of experience having recently come off 24 years of anti-depressants. Barb also has a diploma in Biblical Counselling and Life Coaching. She brings years of experience as well from her Massage Therapy practice where she has pretty much heard it all.

Her personal life's Scripture verse is Isaiah 61:1. "The Spirit of the Lord God is upon Me, because the Lord has anointed Me to preach good tidings to the poor; He has sent Me to heal the brokenhearted, to proclaim liberty to the captives, and the opening of the prison to those who are bound." She is thrilled to be seeing this Scripture coming to fruition in her life.

Barb Tatlock

Barb is married to an absolutely awesome man, whom she feels is a gift from God and lives happily in Airdrie AB.

Made in the USA
Middletown, DE
12 February 2016